QUOTES FOR ATHLETES

A WEEKLY JOURNAL OF QUOTES TO DEVELOP GRIT, MOTIVATION AND A WINNING MINDSET.

THE QUOTIVATION SERIES

DR. JO LUKINS

Copyright © 2025 by Dr. Jo Lukins

All rights reserved.

No part of this book may be reproduced in any form or by any electronic or mechanical means, including information storage and retrieval systems, without written permission from the author, except for the use of brief quotations in a book review.

Names, characters and places have been adapted to share the concepts while protecting the confidentiality of individuals.

ISBN: 978-1-7635127-5-7 (Paperback)

Elite Edge Publishing

www.drjolukins.com

QUOTES FOR ATHLETES INVITES YOU TO EXPLORE WISDOM FROM the world of sports, thoughtfully selected to support your journey. Set aside time each week to reflect on the quote and consider what it means for you. A diary entry or reminder can help you stay committed.

This journal offers space for your weekly reflections. As you consider each quote, notice which ones resonate and which ones you might question. Both reactions help you better understand your values and approach to performance.

The second part of the book provides further reflection questions. These are designed to give you space for your own thoughts before considering additional prompts.

LOOKING FOR SOME EXTRA ACCOUNTABILITY TO KEEP YOU INSPIRED THROUGHOUT THE YEAR?

YOU CAN CHOOSE TO RECEIVE A WEEKLY EMAIL WITH EACH QUOTE AND THE JOURNAL PROMPTS TO HELP YOU STAY MOTIVATED AND ON TRACK. IF YOU'D LIKE TO RECEIVE A WEEKLY REMINDER, SIMPLY SCAN THE QR CODE BELOW AND YOU'LL START GETTING AN EMAIL WITH THE LATEST QUOTE TO HELP YOU MOVE CLOSER TO YOUR GOALS.

The quotes are organised into five key areas of high performance. If you have a particular area you'd like to focus on, use the guide below to find relevant quotes.

Working Hard and Discipline:
Quotes 1, 4, 9, 14, 19, 24, 29, 37, 41. 45, 48, 51

Mindset and Motivation:
Quotes 2, 5, 10, 15, 20, 25, 30, 33, 38, 42, 44, 46, 49, 50, 52

Focus and Preparation:
Quotes 3, 8, 13, 18, 23, 28, 32, 36

Resilience and Overcoming Disappointment:
Quotes 6, 11, 16, 21, 26, 34, 39, 43, 47

Success and Achievement:
Quotes 7, 12, 17, 22, 27, 31, 35, 40

Reflect and Perform

Each page offers a quote to spark reflection about your mindset, routines, and team dynamics. Take your time, revisit the quote over a week, and observe how your views might change with ongoing experience.

Some quotes may be familiar, but their true value comes from thoughtful reflection. Consider how you might apply their message to make a lasting difference in your journey.

Performance-Driven Prompts

- After reflecting, what actions or habits could you apply this week in your sport or preparation?
- If a quote feels at odds with your experience, notice what you believe instead, and let that insight guide you. Importantly, make notes of your wisdom.

In the final section, you'll find space to add quotes you discover throughout the year, allowing your motivation to grow with you.

I look forward to sharing this journey. Reach out to let me know which quotes inspire you, and the impact they have on your performance and mindset. Shine bright, Dr. Jo (excel@drjolukins.com)

CUSTOM COPIES FOR YOUR CLUB, TEAM OR ASSOCIATION
IF YOU'D LIKE YOUR OWN SET OF BOOKS FROM THE QUOTIVATION SERIES, PLEASE CONTACT US ABOUT CREATING A CUSTOM EDITION.

ONE

> Hard work beats talent when talent doesn't work hard.

TIM NOTRE
BASKETBALL COACH WHOSE WISDOM ON EFFORT &
SUCCESS HAS BEEN WIDELY QUOTED BY NBA STARS

TWO

> If you're not willing to risk,
> you cannot grow.
>
> **LES BROWN**
> HALL OF FAME MOTIVATIONAL SPEAKER ON
> OVERCOMING ADVERSITY & PERSONAL DEVELOPMENT
> BESTSELLING AUTHOR

THREE

> A good hockey player plays where the puck is. A great hockey player plays where the puck is going to be.
>
> **WAYNE GRETZKY**
> NHL'S ALL-TIME LEADING SCORER; HOLDS 55 LEAGUE RECORDS; FOUR STANLEY CUPS; *THE GREAT ONE*

FOUR

> Be the hardest-working person you can be. That's how you separate yourself from the competition.
>
> **STEPHEN CURRY**
> FOUR-TIME NBA CHAMPION; TWO-TIME MVP
> DESCRIBED THE GREATEST SHOOTER EVER

FIVE

> If you do not believe you can do it, then you have no chance at all.

ARSENE WENGER

ARSENAL'S MOST SUCCESSFUL MANAGER
TRANSFORMED ENGLISH FOOTBALL AND
REVERED FOR TACTICAL BRILLIANCE

SIX

> As athletes, we have ups and downs. Unfortunately, you can't pick the days they come on.
>
> **DEENA KASTOR**
> OLYMPIC MARATHON MEDALIST;
> HOLDS 10 AMERICAN DISTANCE RUNNING RECORDS

SEVEN

> It's not about being the best. It's about being better than you were yesterday.
>
> **ANGELA DUCKWORTH**
> WORLD EXPERT ON GRIT AND RESILIENCE
> BEST SELLING PSYCHOLOGY AUTHOR AND ACADEMIC

EIGHT

> Behind every kick of a ball, there has to be a thought.
>
> **DENIS BERGKAMP**
> PREMIER LEAGUE LEGEND AND FOOTBALL ICON

NINE

> Gold medals aren't really made of gold. They're made of sweat, determination, and a hard-to-find alloy called guts.
>
> **DAN GABLE**
> OLYMPIC MEDALIST; NCAA COACH; REVERED FOR WORK ETHIC AND INNOVATION IN WRESTLING

TEN

> Start where you are. Use what you have. Do what you can.
> **ARTHUR ASHE**
> GRAND SLAM TENNIS CHAMPION
> HUMANITARIAN LEADER

ELEVEN

> Courage is fear holding on a minute longer.

GEORGE S. PATTON

LEGENDARY WWII US GENERAL; COMMANDER OF KEY ALLIED VICTORIES FAMOUS FOR BOLD STRATEGY AND LEADERSHIP

TWELVE

Success is not about the destination, but the journey.

ZIG ZIGLAR
WORLD-RENOWNED MOTIVATIONAL SPEAKER.
RESPECTED FOR GLOBAL IMPACT, SERVANT
LEADERSHIP & STRONG VALUES

THIRTEEN

> Practice creates confidence.
> Confidence powers you.
>
> **SIMONE BILES**
> MOST DECORATED GYMNAST WITH
> FOUR OLYMPIC GOLD MEDALS

FOURTEEN

> My sports made me a more focused, sharper, determined and stronger person than I was before. It's a mental game: the stronger you are the better you are.
>
> **KIRAN KHAN**
> OLYMPIC SWIMMER
> PAKISTAN'S MULTI-NATIONAL CHAMPION

FIFTEEN

> There is no pressure when you're making a dream come true.
>
> **NEYMAR JR.**
> BRAZIL'S HIGHEST-PROFILE FOOTBALL PLAYER
> FIFA WORLD CUP STAR; RECORD TRANSFER FEE

SIXTEEN

> If you're not making mistakes, then you're not doing anything. I'm positive that a doer makes mistakes.
>
> **JOHN WOODEN**
> 10-TIME NCAA CHAMPION COACH
> LEGENDARY MENTOR AND TEACHER

SEVENTEEN

> Ability is what you're capable of doing. Motivation determines what you do. Attitude determines how well you do it.
>
> **LOU HOLTZ**
> TITLE-WINNING NOTRE DAME FOOTBALL COACH
> MOTIVATIONAL SPEAKER & RESPECTED LEADER

EIGHTEEN

> Football is a game of mistakes. Whoever makes the fewest mistakes wins.
>
> **JOHAN CRUYFF**
> EUROPEAN FOOTBALLER OF THE YEAR
> ARCHITECT OF *TOTAL FOOTBALL*

NINETEEN

> If you want to be the best, you have to do things that other people aren't willing to do.
>
> **MICHAEL PHELPS**
> 23 OLYMPIC GOLDS; MOST DECORATED SWIMMER KNOWN FOR LONGEVITY & DISCIPLINE IN SPORT

TWENTY

> It's so much easier to be yourself than someone else.

ILONA MAHER
RUGBY OLYMPIAN; VIGOROUS
ADVOCATE FOR WOMEN'S SPORT

TWENTY-ONE

> Champions keep playing until they get it right.
>
> **BILLIE JEAN KING**
> SIX-TIME WIMBLEDON CHAMPION

TWENTY-TWO

Success is liking yourself, liking what you do, and liking how you do it.

MAYA ANGELOU
PRESIDENTIAL MEDAL OF FREEDOM WINNER
RENOWNED AUTHOR & POET

TWENTY-THREE

> If you think small things don't matter, think of the last game you lost by one point.
> **UNKNOWN**

TWENTY-FOUR

> "I've worked too hard and too long to let anything stand in the way of my goals.
>
> **TIM HOWARD**
> US SOCCER'S ALL-TIME GREAT GOALKEEPER
> WORLD CUP SAVES RECORD-HOLDER

TWENTY-FIVE

> We become what we think about.
>
> **EARL NIGHTINGALE**
> HALL OF FAME SPEAKER ON GOAL SETTING
> THE VALUE OF POSITIVE THINKING &
> DEFINING SUCCESS

TWENTY-SIX

> I don't run away from a challenge because I am afraid. Instead, I run toward it because the only way to escape fear is to trample it beneath your feet.

NADIA COMANECI
FIRST PERFECT 10 IN OLYMPIC GYMNASTICS
FIVE GOLD MEDALS

TWENTY-SEVEN

> The more difficult the victory, the greater the happiness in winning.
>
> **PELE**
> THREE-TIME WORLD CUP WINNER
> FIFA PLAYER OF THE CENTURY

TWENTY-EIGHT

> The will to win is important, but the will to prepare is vital.
>
> **JOE PATERNO**
> ALL-TIME WINS LEADER IN NCAA FOOTBALL
> COLLEGE FOOTBALL HALL OF FAME COACH

TWENTY-NINE

> You can't get much done in life if you only work on the days when you feel good.

JERRY WEST

NBA HALL OF FAMER
THE 'SILHOUETTE' IN THE NBA LOGO

THIRTY

> The battles that count aren't the ones for gold medals. The struggles within yourself; that's where it's at.
>
> **JESSE OWENS**
> FOUR GOLD MEDALS AT BERLIN OLYMPICS, 1936
> DEFIED THE ODDS AND STOOD AS A SYMBOL
> FOR ATHLETIC COURAGE

THIRTY-ONE

> You have to be able to center yourself, to let all of your emotions go. Don't forget that you play with your soul as well as your body.
>
> **KAREEM ABDUL-JABBAR**
> NBA'S ALL-TIME SCORING LEADER; SIX-TIME MVP
> RESPECTED FOR ACTIVISM & INTELLECTUAL IMPACT

THIRTY-TWO

> The game is won in the mind before it's won on the field.
>
> **EMMITT SMITH**
> NFL CAREER RUSHING RECORD-HOLDER
> THREE SUPERBOWLS

THIRTY-THREE

Winning isn't everything, but wanting to win is.

VINCE LOMBARDI
NFL CHAMPIONSHIP COACH
SUPERBOWL TROPHY NAMESAKE

THIRTY-FOUR

> "What we face may look insurmountable. But I learned something from all those years of training and competing - we are always stronger than we know.
>
> **ARNOLD SCHWARZENEGGER**
> SEVEN MR OLYMPIA TITLES; GLOBAL FITNESS ICON
> AUTHOR, ACTOR & POLITICIAN

THIRTY-FIVE

> The important thing is to learn a lesson every time you lose. Life is a learning process and you have to try to learn what's best for you.
>
> **JOHN McENROE**
> SEVEN GRAND SLAM TITLES; CELEBRATED TV ANALYST KNOWN FOR INTENSITY AND ANALYSIS

THIRTY-SIX

> Effort and courage are not enough without purpose and direction.
>
> **JOHN F. KENNEDY**
> US PRESIDENT RENOWNED FOR VISIONARY LEADERSHIP; INSPIRED NATIONAL FITNESS INITIATIVES

THIRTY-SEVEN

> Discipline is choosing between what you want now with what you want most.
>
> **ABRAHAM LINCOLN**
> US PRESIDENT; LED NATION THROUGH CIVIL WAR
> ENDING SLAVERY; HIGHLY RESPECTED LEGACY

THIRTY-EIGHT

> You don't have to be better than everybody else, you just have to be better than you ever thought you could be.
>
> **KEN VENTURI**
> US OPEN CHAMPION GOLFER

THIRTY-NINE

> I really think a champion is defined not by their wins but by how they can recover when they fall.
>
> **SERENA WILLIAMS**
> 23 GRAND SLAM TITLES; ROLE MODEL FOR ATHLETIC ACHIEVEMENT AND RESILIENCE

FORTY

> It's not who's put up the fastest time in the world that year, or the previous four years, but who can get their hand on the wall first today.
>
> **NATHAN ADRIAN**
> OLYMPIC GOLD MEDALIST

FORTY-ONE

> Repetition is no fun but it's the reason we won.
>
> **MIKE WALDO**
> BASKETBALL HALL OF FAME COACH

FORTY-TWO

> **The most important thing is to try and inspire people so that they can be great in whatever they want to do.**
>
> **KOBE BRYANT**
> FIVE-TIME NBA CHAMPION
> MVP CULTURAL ICON & AUTHOR

FORTY-THREE

> Every strike brings me closer to the next home run.

BABE RUTH
BASEBALL'S GREATEST SLUGGER
HALL OF FAMER

FORTY-FOUR

> Champions never complain, they are too busy getting better.
>
> **JOHN WOODEN**
> LEGENDARY COACH WITH
> 10 NCAA CHAMPIONSHIPS

FORTY-FIVE

> There are no traffic jams along the extra mile.
>
> **ROGER STAUBACH**
> SUPER BOWL MVP
> ICONIC DALLAS COWBOYS QUARTERBACK

FORTY-SIX

You miss 100% of the shots you don't take.

WAYNE GRETZKY
RETIRED HOLDING 61 NHL RECORDS; 9-TIMES MVP

FORTY-SEVEN

> Never give up, never give in, and when the upper hand is ours, may we have the ability to handle the win with the dignity that we absorbed the loss.
>
> **DOUG WILLIAMS**
> FIRST BLACK QUARTERBACK TO WIN SUPERBOWL MVP

FORTY-EIGHT

> Success is no accident. It is hard work, perseverance, learning, studying, sacrifice, and most of all, love of what you are doing.
>
> **PELE**
> GLOBAL SPORT ICON. SO ICONIC HE'S BEEN QUOTED TWICE IN THIS BOOK!

FORTY-NINE

> Our limits may not be where we think they are. Even when we think we've finally reached them, the next time we go there exploring, we often find that they've moved again.

CHRISSIE WELLINGTON
FOUR-TIME IRONMAN WORLD CHAMPION
THE ONLY TRIATHLETE TO WIN A WORLD TITLE
<1 YEAR AFTER TURNING PROFESSIONAL

FIFTY

> You can't fall if you don't climb. But there's no joy in living your whole life on the ground.
>
> **SUSAN KIERNAN-LEWIS**
> AWARD-WINNING AUTHOR

FIFTY-ONE

> Patience is not the ability to wait, but the ability to keep a good attitude while waiting.
>
> **JOYCE MEYER**
> RENOWNED INSPIRATIONAL SPEAKER

FIFTY-TWO

> Do what you can, where you are, with what you have.
>
> **TEDDY ROOSEVELT**
> US PRESIDENT, NOBEL PEACE PRIZE WINNER

You'll find my reflection questions in the following section. They've been included separately so you can first explore your own ideas and see what stands out to you.

As an athlete, this is your chance to stretch your thinking, challenge your habits, and connect each concept to your training and performance in a real and personal way.

Once you've completed your initial reflections, take a moment to read through the additional questions. See what sparks your curiosity or pushes you to think differently. Go back to your earlier notes and build on them; this is where real growth happens.

This process is designed to help you get the most from your reflections and keep your focus on progress, not perfection. Your effort in this space will be reflected in how you show up on the field, in training, and beyond.

DR. JO

ONE

  Hard work beats talent when talent doesn't work hard.

TIM NOTRE

Talent helps, but action is what matters most; consistent hard work will always outpace unused potential. Talent alone is passive, but effort is active and within your control at any moment.

- What stops me from giving full effort every session?
- How can I show that effort matters more than talent?
- When does hard work serve me most, and how do I call on it?

TWO

  If you're not willing to risk, you cannot grow.

LES BROWN

To be willing to risk in order to grow focuses on the value of stepping into uncertainty. Growth occurs at the edges of comfort, through experiences that require courage and vulnerability. Athletes advance by embracing, rather than avoiding, calculated risks.

- Which risks have moved me forward in my personal or athletic development?
- How can I distinguish between helpful risk-taking and recklessness?
- When and why do I hold back from stepping outside my comfort zone?

THREE

> A good hockey player plays where the puck is. A great hockey player plays where the puck is going to be.
>
> WAYNE GRETZKY

Great athletes anticipate what comes next which is a key to sporting intelligence. By preparing for the next moment, you gain a critical edge. Build this skill through intention and regular practice.

- How well do I anticipate opportunities in my sport?
- What helps me read the game or situation ahead of time?
- What is one new habit I can practice for the next four weeks to help build my Sport IQ?

FOUR

> Be the hardest working person you can be. That's how you separate yourself from the competition.
>
> STEPHEN CURRY

Talent is valuable, but effort is something you control and can cultivate every day. Results and personal satisfaction stem from working as hard as you can, regardless of your starting ability.

- What does being the hardest worker look like for me?
- Where could I increase my commitment or focus right now?
- How do I show consistency when motivation drops?

FIVE

 If you do not believe you can do it, then you have no chance at all.

ARSENE WENGER

A winning mindset is built on always striving for success. Avoiding complacency and continually pushing forward keeps your drive sharp and your ambition alive. Relentless belief in yourself is critical.

- When have I performed my best because I believed in myself?
- What doubts might be limiting me before competition?
- How can I strengthen confidence before I perform?

SIX

 As athletes, we have ups and downs. Unfortunately, you can't pick the days they come on.

DEENA KASTOR

The path to reaching goals is rarely smooth, and while it's natural to want control and predictability, true growth comes from how we manage ourselves when things don't go to plan. Confidence comes from our response to each challenge.

- How do I respond on the days when things feel off?
- What helps me reset after a disappointing performance?
- How can I stay balanced when my results fluctuate?

SEVEN

 It's not about being the best. It's about being better than you were yesterday.

ANGELA DUCKWORTH

Progress is best measured by your willingness to improve, not by how you compare yourself to others. When you focus on personal mastery rather than external benchmarks, it's easier to stay motivated and in control.

- What small improvement have I made this week?
- How can I focus on my own growth rather than comparing myself to others?
- What habits can I build today for a better tomorrow?

EIGHT

 Behind every kick of a ball, there has to be a thought.

DENIS BERGKAMP

Even split-second decisions in sport are shaped by your thoughts. Becoming aware of your thinking patterns helps you adjust and find the right balance between overthinking and trusting your instincts. The goal is to use your thoughts as a helpful guide, not a roadblock.

- What's the quality of my focus during performance?
- Which small decisions during play have the biggest impact?
- How could thinking more deliberately improve my game?

NINE

 Gold medals aren't really made of gold. They're made of sweat, determination, and a hard-to-find alloy called guts.

DAN GABLE

Medals represent achievement, but behind each one lies perseverance, grit, and relentless effort. Success comes through these qualities more than through natural talent alone; *guts* means facing challenges head-on and pushing through.

- How do I show determination when things get tough?
- What moments prove I have the courage to persist?
- How can I remind myself that grit fuels achievement?

TEN

 Start where you are. Use what you have. Do what you can.

ARTHUR ASHE

Progress happens when effort is consistent, even if circumstances aren't ideal. We need to make the most of whatever resources, skills, and opportunities are available right now.

- What resources or strengths am I overlooking right now?
- How can I make the most of where I currently am?
- What small, doable step could I take today toward my goal?

ELEVEN

 Courage is fear holding on a minute longer.

GEORGE S. PATTON

Taking risks and facing discomfort, even in small ways, help you grow stronger and build true resilience. Each brave action teaches you something valuable and adds to your confidence.

- When have I persevered by holding on just a little longer?
- What does courage look like when fear shows up in my sport?
- How can I remind myself that bravery begins with persistence?

TWELVE

 Success is not about the destination, but the journey.

ZIG ZIGLAR

Fulfilment is found in the everyday lessons, growth, and commitment, not just the finish line. The process offers opportunities for resilience, adaptation, and joy in everyday commitment. Focusing on the present teaches you to value both setbacks and successes.

- What part of my process do I enjoy the most?
- How do I define success beyond results or outcomes?
- What lessons am I learning while working toward my goals?

THIRTEEN

 Practice creates confidence. Confidence powers you.

SIMONE BILES

Feeling ready to perform is critical to personal confidence. The benefits of focusing on performance not only ensures you are more organised, but gives you controllable actions and personal confidence.

- What does proper preparation look like for me each week?
- How does preparation build trust in my own ability?
- Where could I improve my preparation to strengthen confidence?

FOURTEEN

 My sports made me a more focused, sharper, more determined and stronger person than I was before. It's a mental game—the stronger you are the better you are.

KIRAN KHAN

Sport provides the opportunity to grow mentally and physically, building determination and focus for life. Being challenged reveals the depths of your resilience and sharpness you've gained over time.

- How has sport shaped the person I've become?
- What helps me stay mentally sharp during tough moments?
- How can I train my mind as intentionally as my body?

FIFTEEN

 There is no pressure when you're making a dream come true.

NEYMAR JR.

Gratitude helps transform pressure into positivity on the journey toward your goals. When you treat each step as a privilege, stress fades and you'll enjoy the process more. Smiling through challenges can make the pursuit of your dream rewarding.

- How do I turn pressure into purpose?
- What dream keeps me motivated on hard days?
- How can I see big moments as opportunities, not stress?

SIXTEEN

 If you're not making mistakes, then you're not doing anything. I'm positive that a doer makes mistakes.

JOHN WOODEN

Mistakes are inevitable in sport; the real skill lies in recovering and learning from them. Playing too safely may limit improvement, while repeating errors is part of the journey toward mastery.

- What's a recent mistake that taught me something valuable?
- How can I approach mistakes as part of growth?
- How do I keep taking action even when I fear getting it wrong?

SEVENTEEN

> Ability is what you're capable of doing. Motivation determines what you do. Attitude determines how well you do it.
>
> LOU HOLTZ

Talent gets you started, but mindset and motivation turn potential into achievement. Success is built on skill, attitude, and persistence working together.

- Which of these—ability, motivation, or attitude—needs my attention most right now?
- How does my attitude impact my performance and environment?
- What motivates me even when ability alone isn't enough?

EIGHTEEN

> Football is a game of mistakes. Whoever makes the fewest mistakes wins.
>
> JOHAN CRUYFF

Mistakes are part of every athlete's journey and offer powerful learning experiences. The better you understand your sport, the more skilled you become at handling setbacks and minimizing errors.

- How do I limit errors without fearing them?
- What helps me recover quickly after a mistake?
- How do I learn from errors to improve next time?

NINETEEN

 If you want to be the best, you have to do things that other people aren't willing to do.

MICHAEL PHELPS

Every day involves choices about whether to take the extra step toward excellence. The willingness to do hard or unpopular work distinguishes those who reach greatness from those who do not.

- What extra step could I take that others might avoid?
- How do I stay disciplined when no one's watching?
- How does doing hard things make me different from the rest?

TWENTY

 It's so much easier to be yourself than someone else.

ILONA MAHER

Authenticity takes less energy than being pretentious. When we try to imitate others, we waste focus and create unnecessary pressure. True confidence and freedom in performance come from trusting who we are and bringing that self to every moment.

- Where do I feel most confident being fully myself?
- When have I performed best by staying authentic?
- How can I bring more of my true self to competition?

TWENTY-ONE

 Champions keep playing until they get it right.

BILLIE JEAN KING

Effort and perseverance reveal an athlete's true passion for their craft. The pathway to improvement lies in pushing forward, even when progress feels slow.

- What keeps me practicing when improvement feels slow?
- How can patience support my pursuit of mastery?
- When have I grown most because I refused to quit?

TWENTY-TWO

 Success is liking yourself, liking what you do, and liking how you do it.

MAYA ANGELOU

Achievement is not only about public recognition but also the satisfaction found in your own journey. This mindset invites you to define success on your own terms, independent of outside approval.

- What do I appreciate most about who I am right now?
- How do I find joy in the process of competing and learning?
- What habits help me like how I approach my goals?

TWENTY-THREE

> If you think small things don't matter, think of the last game you lost by one point.
>
> UNKNOWN

Success in sport is often decided by the smallest margins. Focusing on the little details creates a ripple effect, influencing performance far beyond the moment. Careful attention to these moments ensures no opportunity for improvement is missed on the path to your goals.

- What small detail could have changed a past performance?
- How does consistency in little things build big results?
- What small action could make a difference this week?

TWENTY-FOUR

> I've worked too hard and too long to let anything stand in the way of my goals.
>
> TIM HOWARD

Big achievements demand sustained effort and commitment over time. On difficult days, remembering your dedication can help you overcome barriers and stay focused on your long-term aspirations.

- When have I overcome obstacles through sheer persistence?
- What motivates me to keep pushing through setbacks?
- How can I protect my focus from distractions around me?

TWENTY-FIVE

 We become what we think about.

EARL NIGHTINGALE

The thoughts you focus on shape your reality, habits, and identity. A positive, performance-focused mindset creates the conditions for achievement. Your beliefs guide your actions, so choose them wisely.

- Are my thoughts helping or hindering my progress?
- What self-beliefs do I want to strengthen in my game?
- How can I train my mindset as I train my body?

TWENTY-SIX

 I don't run away from a challenge because I am afraid. Instead, I run toward it because the only way to escape fear is to trample it beneath your feet.

NADIA COMANECI

Everyone experiences fear, but what matters most is how you think about it. Feeling fear may be guiding you to step back or away, or challenging you to step forward.

- What challenge could I face head-on right now?
- When did I last turn fear into motivation?
- How can I treat fear as a sign I'm growing?

TWENTY-SEVEN

 The more difficult the victory, the greater the happiness in winning.

PELE

Challenges shape both mental and physical strength, making success feel much more rewarding. Knowing that the path was tough adds meaning to every achievement.

- What tough victories have felt most rewarding to me?
- How does struggle make success more meaningful?
- How can I stay patient when success feels far away?

TWENTY-EIGHT

 The will to win is important, but the will to prepare is vital.

JOE PATERNO

Whilst many are driven by victory, champions draw motivation from the journey itself. Consistency and enthusiasm when preparing, leads to both resilience and success.

- How consistent is my preparation under pressure?
- What does exceptional preparation look like for me?
- How can I better align preparation with my goals?

TWENTY-NINE

 You can't get much done in life if you only work on the days when you feel good.

JERRY WEST

Consistency trumps circumstances; true progress results from showing up even when motivation is low. Great habits are built during difficult days, not just the easy ones.

- How can I perform regardless of how I feel?
- What habits keep me consistent on low-energy days?
- What pushes me to show up even when it's tough?

THIRTY

 The battles that count aren't the ones for gold medals. The struggles within yourself—that's where it's at.

JESSE OWENS

Progress is made one step at a time, using the resources and abilities available to you right now. You do not need perfect conditions to move forward; consistent practical action builds momentum for lasting improvement.

- What internal battles am I currently facing as an athlete?
- How do I strengthen mental control under stress?
- What helps me win the small battles each day?

THIRTY-ONE

 You have to be able to center yourself, to let all of your emotions go. Don't forget that you play with your soul as well as your body.

KAREEM ABDUL-JABBAR

Performing at your peak requires setting aside distracting emotions and focusing on the present moment. When you connect your mind and body, you play with greater confidence and joy.

- How do I reconnect with joy and purpose in sport?
- What helps me stay composed when emotions rise?
- How can I bring more soul and presence into my game?

THIRTY-TWO

 The game is won in the mind before it's won on the field.

EMMITT SMITH

Mental preparation sets the tone for your confidence and performance. Directing your thoughts in helpful ways gives you a competitive advantage.

- What helpful thinking is best for your next competition?
- What strategies help you switch off when you need a break from thinking about competition?
- When unhelpful thoughts show up, how will you choose to respond?

THIRTY-THREE

  Winning isn't everything, but wanting to win is.

VINCE LOMBARDI

The drive and desire to pursue victory, is as much quest as the result. Motivation to win stimulates effort and persistence, laying the foundation for success even in the face of setbacks.

- How can I channel my drive to win positively?
- When does my competitive spirit bring out my best?
- What motivates me most when I compete?

THIRTY-FOUR

  What we face may look insurmountable. But I learned something from all those years of training and competing - we are always stronger than we know.

ARNOLD SCHWARZENEGGER

Challenges often seem greater than our resources, but repeated effort reveals hidden reserves of strength. Recognizing your capability builds confidence for the next test you face.

- When have I proven I'm stronger than expected?
- What reminds me of my resilience in hard times?
- How can I keep uncovering hidden strength?

THIRTY-FIVE

 The important thing is to learn a lesson every time you lose. Life is a learning process and you have to try to learn what's best for you.

JOHN MCENROE

Defeat and setbacks are inevitable, but they offer valuable lessons. Growth happens when you reflect, adapt, and keep moving forward despite disappointment. Each experience, win or lose, builds wisdom.

- How do I handle losses productively?
- What did my last setback teach me?
- How can I turn frustration into growth?

THIRTY-SIX

 Effort and courage are not enough without purpose and direction.

JOHN F. KENNEDY

If we think of effort and courage as the engine room of our performance; purpose and direction are the compass that steers us in the right direction. Bravery plays an important role in how well we perform, yet its impact is limited without clear goals.

- What fuels my purpose as an athlete right now?
- How can I align my effort with a clear direction?
- When have I competed with focus and true intent?

THIRTY-SEVEN

 Discipline is choosing between what you want now with what you want most.

ABRAHAM LINCOLN

Greatness results from consistently prioritizing long-term goals. Discipline is a skill you strengthen through ongoing, intentional choices. Each time you choose growth, your mental resolve increases.

- What daily choices bring me closer to my biggest goal?
- Which short-term temptations slow my progress?
- How can I practice daily discipline with intention?

THIRTY-EIGHT

 You don't have to be better than everybody else, you just have to be better than you ever thought you could be.

KEN VENTURI

Progress comes from surpassing your own limits, not just comparing yourself to others. Setting internal benchmarks and aiming to outdo your past accomplishments unlocks your greatest potential.

- What does personal best mean to me today?
- Where have I outperformed my old self lately?
- How can I redefine progress based on my journey?

THIRTY-NINE

> I really think a champion is defined not by their wins but by how they can recover when they fall.
>
> SERENA WILLIAMS

Persistent effort transforms setbacks into stepping stones for future success. Lasting achievement comes from continual effort, adaptation, and the refusal to give up even when progress is slow.

- What does recovery look like for me after failure?
- Who supports me most when I stumble?
- How can I bounce back even stronger next time?

FORTY

> It's not who's put up the fastest time in the world that year, or the previous four years, but who can get their hand on the wall first today.
>
> NATHAN ADRIAN

Winning requires you to focus fully on the present and channel all your energy into what counts right now. By letting go of past results, you can prepare your mind and body to give your best today.

- How can I stay fully focused on the present moment?
- When do I get distracted by others' achievements?
- How will I compete *in the now* next time?

FORTY-ONE

 Repetition is no fun but it's the reason we won.

MIKE WALDO

Success comes through practice and repetition, even when it's tedious or dull. Repeating a skill builds muscle memory, freeing up your mind for critical moments in competition.

- What daily repetitions matter most for my improvement?
- How do I keep motivation through routine practice?
- When has repetition directly led to success?

FORTY-TWO

 The most important thing is to try and inspire people so that they can be great in whatever they want to do.

KOBE BRYANT

Inspiring others is a powerful legacy, extending the impact of your achievements beyond yourself. Supporting and uplifting those around you broadens your sense of purpose and builds a lasting influence within and outside your sport. Strive to be a source of motivation and encouragement for others.

- How can I use my example to inspire others?
- What qualities do I admire in others?
- What does leadership through action mean to me?

FORTY-THREE

 Every strike brings me closer to the next home run.

BABE RUTH

Disappointment is a natural part of competing, but each setback offers lessons to improve for next time. How you interpret moments of disappointment matters more than the disappointment itself.

- What setbacks are preparing me for future wins?
- How can I stay persistent through repeated failure?
- What helps me believe in progress despite mistakes?

FORTY-FOUR

 Champions never complain, they are too busy getting better.

JOHN WOODEN

Success is rarely found by those who make a habit of complaining. Developing a mindset of gratitude enhances performance and helps redirect frustration into progress. Rather than being sidetracked by setbacks, focus on improvement through a performance mindset.

- How can I focus on solutions, not excuses?
- When have I redirected frustration into improvement?
- What can I work on quietly today to get better?

FORTY-FIVE

   There are no traffic jams along the extra mile.

ROGER STAUBACH

Exceptional effort is rare, allowing those who push further to stand out and achieve what others cannot. Going beyond what is required can set a personal standard and lead to unique rewards and growth.

- What does going the extra mile look like in my sport?
- What keeps me committed when others slow down?
- When have I seen effort give me an advantage?

FORTY-SIX

   You miss 100% of the shots you don't take.

WAYNE GRETZKY

Opportunity only arises when you are willing to try, regardless of the outcome. If you don't step forward, you lose your chance by default. Choosing bravery even with uncertain results is essential for growth.

- What opportunities am I hesitating to pursue?
- How can I replace fear with action?
- What could I gain by just taking the next shot?

FORTY-SEVEN

 Never give up, never give in, and when the upper hand is ours, may we have the ability to handle the win with the dignity that we absorbed the loss.

DOUG WILLIAMS

Greatness is revealed in both victory and defeat, and true growth comes from the humility with which we approach both. Dignity in all outcomes builds lasting strength and character.

- How do I demonstrate grace in victory and defeat?
- What keeps me resilient when things go wrong?
- How can I win humbly and lose with dignity?

FORTY-EIGHT

 Success is no accident. It is hard work, perseverance, learning, studying, sacrifice, and most of all, love of what you are doing.

PELE

Lasting achievement arises from hard work, commitment, and passion for the craft. Adversity and sacrifice are necessary in the journey toward fulfilling pursuits, but loving your work sustains you.

- What part of my work reflects true love for my sport?
- How can I sustain effort through both joy and struggle?
- What sacrifices highlight my dedication to this path?

FORTY-NINE

 Our limits may not be where we think they are. Even when we think we've finally reached them, the next time we go there exploring, we often find that they've moved again.

CHRISSIE WELLINGTON

Our greatest test is within; your thoughts and actions challenge you more than opponents. How you talk to yourself shapes your performance. Master positive self-talk to become your own best advocate.

- When was I last surprised by doing more than expected?
- How can I use discomfort to expand my limits?
- What routine could help me keep exploring my potential?

FIFTY

 You can't fall if you don't climb. But there's no joy in living your whole life on the ground.

SUSAN KIERNAN-LEWIS

Growth requires a willingness to take risks and embrace challenges. Staying in your comfort zone may keep you safe, but it limits your achievement. Each climb brings new opportunities to embrace.

- Where am I avoiding challenge out of comfort?
- When did I last feel joy from taking a bold step?
- How can I climb higher in my sport or mindset?

FIFTY-ONE

> Patience is not the ability to wait, but the ability to keep a good attitude while waiting.
>
> JOYCE MEYER

Patience is essential for long-term success; when we recognize that worthwhile goals take time, we can embrace the journey and avoid becoming discouraged by delays. Steady progress often requires managing frustration, which signals growth and improvement.

- What helps me stay positive during long processes?
- When has patience led to great results for me?
- How can I practice gratitude while waiting for progress?

FIFTY-TWO

> Do what you can, where you are, with what you have.
>
> TEDDY ROOSEVELT

The best any of us can attain is to do whatever is within our relative levels of energy, in this moment, with our current resources. Be kind to yourself and understand that if you are feeling 70%, then giving 70% is 100%!

- How can I make the most of my current situation?
- What can I do today to move one step forward?
- How does focusing on what I have empower me?

OTHER QUOTES TO INSPIRE

Use this section to collect quotes that inspire you throughout the year. Add a few notes about why each quote stands out or what it means to you personally.

To read more from the Quotivation series

The Quotivation Series is a collection of reflective quote journals designed to take short bites of wisdom, and applying it in a practical way to your upcoming success.

Quotes for Athletes: *A weekly journal of quotes for grit, motivation and a winning mindset.*
Quotes for Coaches: *A weekly journal of quotes for leadership, motivation and excellence.*
Quotes for Referees: *A weekly journal of quotes for focus, poise and resilience.*
Quotes for Business: *A weekly journal of quotes for strategy, growth and success.*
Quotes for Leaders: *A weekly journal of quotes for vision, courage, and inspired achievement.*
Quotes for Investors: *A weekly journal of quotes for patience, clarity and a successful investors mindset.*
Quotes for Military: *A weekly journal of quotes for courage, discipline, and an unbreakable mindset in service.*
Quotes for Parenting: *A weekly journal of quotes for patience, guidance, and love.*
Quotes for Students: *A weekly journal of quotes for focus, persistence and curiosity.*
Quotes for You: *A weekly journal of quotes for growth, self-discovery, and an empowered mindset.*

The Quotivation Series is being released through 2026.
Visit my website **drjolukins.com** to be the first to order your copy or visit your preferred indie bookstore or online platform.

CUSTOM COPIES FOR YOUR TEAM OR BUSINESS

IF YOU'D LIKE TO SHARE A BOOK FROM THE QUOTIVATION SERIES WITH A CLUB, ASSOCIATION OR TEAM, PLEASE CONTACT US TO DISCUSS CREATING A CUSTOM EDITION.

EMAIL US AT **EXCEL@DRJOLUKINS.COM** TO FIND OUT MORE.

THE QUOTIVATION SERIES

QUOTES for ATHLETES

A weekly journal of quotes to develop grit, motivation and a winning mindset.

DR. JO LUKINS

READ MORE WITH DR. JO

The following books are available at your favourite book store or online platform:

The Elite: Think like an athlete, succeed like a champion. Ten things the elite do differently. 2019

In the Grandstands: The sporting parents guide to raising a confident and happy teen in the highs and lows of youth sports. 2020

The Game Plan: Your 5-month coaching program to champion high performance habits (High Performance Thinking). 2022

The Elite and The Game Plan 2 in 1 Book: Champion your success with elite habits to unleash your winning potential with 10 proven strategies and high-performance coaching program. 2023

Belief: Building unshakeable confidence. 2024

The Whistle Blower: The mental toughness rulebook for referees, umpires, and sports officials. 2025.

The Whistle Blower Workbook: The mental toughness rulebook for referees, umpires, and sports officials. 2025

A note from Dr. Jo

Referred to as a psychological Indiana Jones, thanks to more than twenty-five years spent exploring what helps people achieve their best. I have enjoyed bringing together these quotes for you. If you'd like to connect or learn more, you can always find me at www.drjolukins.com.

If Quotes for Athletes has made an impact for you, I'd be grateful if you would share your thoughts or leave a review. Similarly, if you'd like to share your favorite quote with me, let me know at excel@drjolukins.com

Shine Bright, Dr. Jo

www.ingramcontent.com/pod-product-compliance
Lightning Source LLC
Chambersburg PA
CBHW071854070526
44583CB00016B/1682